WILLIAM J.
BAROODY, SR.

The Francis Boyer Lectures on Public Policy

WILLIAM J. BAROODY, SR.

Recipient of the 1980 Boyer Award

Remembered by

Paul W. McCracken
Robert H. Bork
Irving Kristol
Michael Novak

American Enterprise Institute for Public Policy Research

ISBN 0-8447-1355-4

Library of Congress Catalog Card No. 81-71261

American Enterprise Institute for Public Policy Research
1150 Seventeenth Street, N.W., Washington, D.C. 20036

CONTENTS

THE
FRANCIS BOYER LECTURES
ON PUBLIC POLICY

The American Enterprise Institute has initiated the Francis Boyer Lectures on Public Policy to examine the relationship between business and government and to develop contexts for their creative interaction. These lectures have been made possible by an endowment from the SmithKline Corporation in memory of Mr. Boyer, the late chairman of the board of the corporation.

The lecture is given by an eminent thinker who has developed notable insights on one or more aspects of the relationship between the nation's private and public sectors. Focusing clearly on the public interest, the lecture demonstrates how new conceptual insights may illuminate public policy issues and contribute significantly to the dialogue by which the public interest is served.

The man or woman delivering the lecture need not necessarily be a professional scholar, a government official, or a business leader. The lecture would concern itself with the central issues of public policy in contemporary America—pointing always in the direction of constructive solutions rather than merely delineating opposing views.

Lecturers may come from any walk of life—academia, the humanities, public service, science, finance, the mass media of communications, business, and industry. The principal considerations determining the selection are the quality and appositeness of the lecturer's thought, rather than his or her formal qualifications.

The Francis Boyer Lecture is delivered annually in Washington, D.C., before an invited audience. The lecturer is selected by the American Enterprise Institute's distinguished Council of Academic Advisers, and the lectureship carries an award and stipend of $10,000. The American Enterprise Institute publishes the lecture as the Francis Boyer Lectures on Public Policy.

The initial recipient of the Francis Boyer award was Gerald R. Ford, thirty-eighth president of the United States and the Distinguished Fellow of the American Enterprise Institute.

The second recipient of the award was Dr. Arthur F. Burns, Distinguished Scholar in Residence at the American Enterprise Institute.

The third recipient was Paul Johnson, the former editor of the *New Statesman* and the author of *Enemies of Society*, *A History of Christianity*, and *Elizabeth I: A Study in Power and Intellect*.

PREFACE

Competition of ideas is fundamental to a free society. A free society, if it is to remain free, cannot permit itself to be dominated by one strain of thought.

WILLIAM J. BAROODY, SR., 1916–1980

The 1980 recipient of the Francis Boyer award, William J. Baroody, Sr., was chosen by the American Enterprise Institute's Council of Academic Advisers in May 1980. He was selected because of his lifetime of dedication to the competition of ideas, a competition he believed essential to the formation of public policy.

To that end, he took a faltering organization, which he joined in 1954, and invested his tireless energy, his wisdom, his amazing intellectual capacity, and his boundless love for humanity, and built it into a significant force in public policy research: the American Enterprise Institute for Public Policy Research.

Had he lived, we would present here his own message, his own evaluation of the relationship between the public and private sectors of our society. He gave much thought to that relationship, and to the values generated by the private institutions of society—family, church, neighborhood, voluntary associations, ethnic groups, the workplace, and other organizations to which people gravitate to fulfill their needs. He believed that public policy must *undergird*, not *undermine*, those values and those institutions. And he believed that a public policy which does not reflect those fundamental values would in time fail.

We cannot print those insights here, because he died on July 28, 1980. His message to us must be found in the kind of institution he created, a place for scholars who are willing to go beyond the common wisdom to look for new challenges, new ideas, new visions of our society.

To present the Francis Boyer Lecture in his honor, the Council of Academic Advisers asked four such scholars, four men who surely fit our oft-stated guidelines for the Francis Boyer lecturer: "an eminent thinker who has developed notable insights on one or more aspects of the relationship between the Nation's private and public sectors."

All four are great and distinguished experts on public policy; all four were close personal friends of my father. Each was chosen to present insights in the four areas of public policy to which my father devoted most of his energy:

• On the *economy*, Paul W. McCracken, chairman of the Council of Academic Advisers at AEI and Edmund Ezra Day University Professor of Business Administration at the University of Michigan

• On *social philosophy*, Irving Kristol, senior fellow of AEI and professor of social thought at New York University

• On *religion and public policy*, Michael Novak, AEI resident scholar in religion, philosophy and public policy

• And on the *law*, Robert H. Bork, a member of the AEI Council of Academic Advisers and then Alexander M. Bickel

Professor of Public Law at Yale Law School (who was unable to deliver his address at the annual Public Policy Dinner because of the untimely death of his beloved wife, Claire, but whose text is included in this volume).

Also presented in this volume are the remarks of then-President-elect Ronald W. Reagan and former President Gerald R. Ford on December 11, 1980, at AEI's annual Public Policy Dinner in Washington, D.C., at which the Boyer lecture traditionally is delivered.

The story of William J. Baroody, Sr., is an American story: the son of an immigrant Lebanese stonecutter who grows up to mingle with national leaders and put his stamp firmly on the public policy process for much of his life and for the years to come. He has left us a profound legacy; our challenge is to live up to it.

Bill Baroody Jr.

WILLIAM J. BAROODY, JR.

President
American Enterprise Institute

WILLIAM J. BAROODY, SR.

Remembered by
Paul W. McCracken

This year's nominee for the Francis Boyer lecture and award is in a very real sense an active participant in our evening's program. That is, of course, true in the quite obvious sense that if Bill Baroody, Sr., had focused his formidable combination of intellectual and organizational talents in other directions, there would not be the AEI that exists today as a major center of intellectual activity, and you and I this evening would have no reason (or at least would not have this reason) for being here at all.

Bill Baroody, Sr., is, however, an active participant this evening in what can be considered a more fundamental sense. This organization under whose auspices we meet has been built on the foundation of two related convictions. First, what goes on in the idea world ultimately shapes public policy. Second, if there is genuinely free competition in the marketplace of ideas, good policies will be the ultimate result of this process.

That each period's agenda of public policy issues bears the stamp of earlier activity in the world of ideas has long been recognized. We are all familiar with the observation of Lord Keynes: "the ideas of economists and political philosophers, both when they are right and when they are wrong, are more powerful than commonly understood. Indeed, the world is ruled by little else."[1]

While even his critics would not accuse Keynes of any inability to think original thoughts, Keynes's comment was possibly a lineal descendant from his teacher, Alfred Marshall of Cambridge, who wrote in his *Principles of Economics* (which became required reading for generations of aspiring economists): "the full importance of an epoch-making idea is often not perceived in the generation in which it is made: it starts the thoughts of the world on a new track, but the change of direction is not obvious until the turning point has been left some way behind."[2]

When the history of economic policy during the middle third of this century is finally written, it will, I believe, be recorded that the outer limits of permissible thinking had narrowed to the danger point. The economy, we came to believe, could be managed through maneuvering the government's fiscal operations, and the suggestion, and the person making the suggestion, that money and monetary policy matter deserved and received the treatment usually accorded to heresies and heretics. Services provided through government are Good, and things provided by the private sector are Tail Fins. The results have been predictable. The reach and scope of government greatly enlarged. Questions have been seriously raised, with a continuation of this trend, about the dangers to a liberal order, not from some man on a horse, but from a conviction that our lives

[1] J. M. Keynes, *The General Theory of Employment, Interest, and Money* (Harcourt, Brace, 1935), p. 383.
[2] Alfred Marshall, *Principles of Economics*, 8th ed. (London: Macmillan, 1952), p. 70.

were being hopelessly enmeshed in a bureaucracy not controlled either by the citizenry or by its elected officials. The performance of the economy has deteriorated. It has become, relative to its historical record, more unstable, more inflationary, less capable of delivering gains in real income, and more inclined to operate at lower levels of employment.

Fortunately, an invigorated competition in the market-place of ideas has also emerged, and the intellectual spectrum shaping the formation of economic policy has broadened. The economics profession, which once almost unanimously assumed the virtual irrelevance of monetary policy, is now consuming tons of journal paper with articles and studies which seem to agree that money at least matters. The once-popular public-poverty–private-affluence view has given way to analytical studies of program benefits and program costs. The view that a government-directed economic system is the wave of the future is now seen to be the warmed-over economics of Colbert, who lived a century before Adam Smith, and it has worked no better for us than for Louis XIV.

The American Enterprise Institute for Public Policy Research cannot claim single-handedly to have wrought this change, but its becoming of major league size more than a decade ago clearly made a difference. And AEI made a difference in part because its commitment to the importance for a free society of the competition of ideas helped to release us from the narrowing boundaries of the old establishmentarian thinking.

Our economic future may therefore be more promising than we now, in the midst of dislocations and imbalances that have long persisted, would be prepared to believe. What in more concrete and practical terms is this apt to mean for the economic environment in which we make a living, manage our businesses, and pursue our careers in government?

For one thing, the 1980s have a good chance now of being the decade during which the American price level returns to the greater degree of stability that has been characteristic of our history. The old establishmentarian view of this century's middle years, that yet a little more inflation should be accepted as the cost of yet lower rates of unemployment, is now seen to be a loser. The result then is higher rates of both inflation and unemployment—with those at the outer margin of the labor force bearing a disproportionate burden from this misguided strategy.

The probability is high that the 1980s will also see the U.S. economy recover its lost capability to deliver gains in productivity and therefore in real incomes. The nation now sees that there are no disembodied entities called corporations on whom tax burdens can be imposed. Only people pay taxes. Our efforts during this century's middle years to evade this point has given us the low-profit and low-investment economy, with its attendant aging technology, that has in turn imposed on Americans static-to-declining real incomes. A major reorientation of these policies toward a high-investment economy will almost certainly begin in 1981.

A high-investment economy means, by the inexorable logic of double-entry statistics, a high-savings economy. And that will mean that the relaxed views about the growth of the federal budget and the size of its deficits, which characterized the century's middle years, will change. Deficits relative to GNP that can be readily carried by high-savings economies, such as Japan and the Federal Republic of Germany, will not do for us. After the Treasury has satisfied its borrowing requirements, too little of the more limited flow of funds into credit markets becomes available for financing capital formation, housing, and auto sales. Public budgets and deficits will find themselves in the years ahead on a shorter leash and requiring far more effective fiscal management.

Finally, the drift of this century's middle years toward

government management of the details of economic life is changing, and the new trend is toward a liberal, market-organized economic strategy. In part, this sea-change reflects the incontestable evidence of experience both here and abroad. State-managed economies, where we see in their least ambiguous form the results when government explicitly operates the economy, are this era's economic failure stories. Two recent pictures in American newspapers capture this verdict of experience. After six decades, a span of time equal to that from our own Civil War to the mid-1920s, we see long queues of Russians hoping to buy some sausage. And we see crowds gather before a store in Warsaw hoping to buy some butter. These are not vignettes of economic progress.

In 1919, Justice Oliver Wendell Holmes, Jr., observed:

> When men have realized that time has upset many
> fighting faiths, they may come to believe even more
> than they believe the very foundations of their own
> conduct that the ultimate good desired is better reached
> by free trade in ideas—that the best test of truth is
> the power of the thought to get itself accepted in the
> competition of the market.[3]

It is the ascendancy in the intellectual marketplace of new ideas about public policy that gives us, at a time when our economic problems are so formidable, reassuring auguries of things to come.

[3] In his opinion, Abrams v. United States, 1919.

WILLIAM J. BAROODY, SR.

Remembered by
Robert H. Bork

For those who have not known the American Enterprise Institute long, it is probably difficult to grasp the magnitude of the accomplishment of Bill Baroody, Sr. AEI existed before Bill took over its leadership, but it was not merely tiny and without pretension, it was virtually defunct—financially and intellectually. Only a man of very considerable vision and irrepressible optimism could have imagined that AEI could be revitalized as a major center of intellectual force brought to bear upon the formation and implementation of public policy.

Bill, of course, was precisely such a man. When I first met him in 1964, the rejuvenation of AEI was in full swing. The memory of that first meeting is important to me, largely because Bill became a good and valued friend but also because his qualities determined the character of the institution we know today. If it is ever true that an institution is the shadow of a single man, it is true of AEI and Bill Baroody. This is as much a matter of personality and character as of intellect and organizational ability. At our first meeting, Bill struck me as genial, cheerful, and tough-minded. Over time, I came to see him also as sympathetic and immensely loyal to old friends and allies. I think that one may discern these qualities today in the tone and morale of AEI. These attributes do more than provide a pleasant atmosphere, they make interaction freer and work more productive. These are elusive concepts, impossible to demonstrate, but anyone who has spent much time in a university or a research institute knows their importance.

Equally important and evident was Bill's skill as an impresario of ideas and of intellectual talent. The staff in Washington was of high quality but quite small; it took only a short time to meet everybody on the premises. But Bill and that staff worked assiduously to locate those men and women on campuses around the country who should be associated with AEI. The advisory board already contained men like Paul McCracken, Milton Friedman, and Gottfried Haberler, and many others then less well known produced studies and analyses of uniformly high quality.

Assembling that pool of talent cannot have been easy. Though there was never a party line at AEI, there was a theme, as you might guess from the three economists just named. In general, AEI's values were traditional, and its scholars tended, where possible, to devise voluntary or market, rather than statist, approaches to public policy issues. This was a sharp contrast to the consensus on most campuses at the time.

AEI became a focal point for academics of roughly compatible viewpoints. Persons who often, particularly in those years, felt intellectually isolated, even beleaguered, on their own campuses were drawn into a larger intellectual community. But for AEI, many of them might not have known the reinforcing and invigorating effect such a community can produce.

Though AEI's strength historically has been in economics, Bill Baroody understood that a healthy polity requires much more than a sound economic policy. It is for that reason that

AEI scholars are to be found working in every discipline that relates to public policy.

Law and the performance of courts have become a particular source of policy controversy. The federal judiciary of the United States have always been the most powerful and active in the world. That is true, of course, because for a long time only this nation had a tradition of judicial review under the Constitution. In the past quarter of a century, American courts have become more dominant, more activist, more managerial than ever before. Few aspects of American life have been un-affected by judicial decisions and decrees.

Activist courts are not new in our history. For over half a century federal courts, without an adequate warrant in the Constitution, struck down state and federal laws that infringed too far, in the courts' view, on the rights of property and on business freedom. That era came to a sharp and dramatic close with Franklin Roosevelt's assault upon the Supreme Court through the Court-packing plan. Though Roosevelt's assault miscarried, the judiciary were chastened and entered upon a period of self-restraint.

In retrospect, it appears that much of what appeared to be an objection to excessive government by the judiciary was not that at all but an objection to the political ends the judiciary served. Throughout the brief era of relative self-restraint, a strong school of thought urged courts on to adventures in a different direction. That school ultimately achieved dominance with the Warren Court. That Court was egalitarian, and its constitutional rulings served constituencies of the New Deal. Some of those rulings could have been justified on conventional constitutional grounds; many could not.

Perhaps the most important fact about the Warren Court was not the political direction of its rulings but its establishment of a new model of judicial behavior. Even the pre–New Deal courts had never legislated so freely on so many topics as did the Warren Court. Moreover, the judges learned that the opposition of the political branches and the public was less to be feared than they had thought. The political process seemed able to make no effective response even to the Court's most outrageous *ipse dixits*.

The Warren Court has passed into history. New judges do not share all of its political agenda. But, whatever the content, the style of judging remains with us. The Burger Court is no less inclined to starkly legislative judging, and that style has been adopted by many lower federal courts and by some state court systems. This is not alone a matter of the creation of new constitutional rights out of no more legitimate sources than the judges' social and political sympathies. It extends to the interpretation of statutes to accomplish judicially favored ends that the legislators never intended or, in some cases, affirmatively repudiated.

The new style extends well beyond the announcement of new and unsupportable legal rules; it includes a willingness, even an eagerness, to wrest the management of major institutions from other branches of government. It is now routine for judges to manage school systems, prisons, mental hospitals, fire departments, and so on. Courts are not good managers; in many instances they are disastrous managers; but there seems no way for the public to get their institutions back into the hands of their representatives. The aggressiveness and assumed omnicompetence of our courts today was unthought of and unthinkable thirty years ago. There is no very good reason to think these qualities are at their apogee or that courts will not have taken over still more of our lives ten or twenty years hence.

If anything halts this trend, it is likely to be the political reaction now growing in the country. The reaction is understandable, in many ways even laudable, but it suffers from severe defects and handicaps. For one thing, it is rather narrowly focused on a few subjects where the courts have assailed the values of particular constituencies. The political reaction, therefore, does not address anything like the full range of judicial usurpations of power.

Moreover, the political process has few effective weapons with which to respond to the courts. Devices such as the removal of jurisdiction are mooted, but this is troublesome in principle and ineffective in practice. Removal of the Supreme Court's appellate jurisdiction in a particular class of cases, even if one assumes the constitutionality of the tactic and the Court's acquiescence, would overturn the historic relationships between the branches. It would not return power to democratic processes, but would lodge it in state courts, and the device can hardly be employed in all the areas in which the Court has wrongfully assumed power.

We have reached a state of crisis in democratic government, a crisis brought on by the courts, and we seem to lack a solution for it. Indeed, because many lawyers and legal intellectuals prefer the results attainable through courts to the processes of democracy, we lack even general agreement that anything is out of kilter.

In this state of affairs, perhaps the best, because the only, thing to do is to focus and accelerate the debate about the proper function of courts in our system of government. This is a task to which AEI is contributing greatly through conferences and publications. There are times when it seems impossible that we will ever achieve even a rough consensus. The subject does not lend itself to logic with the rigor of economic reasoning, and powerful elements of the legal community have strong interests in judicial imperialism. Nonetheless, other public policy arguments that seemed hopeless have been won over a period of years or decades. It is quite possible that this one will be, too; if it is, AEI will have provided an important impetus and forum. Both of those exist because of Bill Baroody. Here, as elsewhere, his life's work is still in the process of completion.

WILLIAM J. BAROODY, SR.

Remembered by

Irving Kristol

It is a truth generally acknowledged that, the older one is, the less the likelihood of acquiring good and close friends. I count myself fortunate in having experienced some exceptions to this rule, and easily the most exceptional exception was my friendship with Bill Baroody, Sr., struck up seven years before his untimely death.

We hit it off from the very first encounter, at which, I recall, a discussion of the political and economic scene was quickly elevated to an analysis of our cultural condition and, with only a slight delay, briskly proceeded in a still more abstract direction, to an intense and lengthy dialogue about the crisis in political philosophy that threatened the foundations of Western civilization, no less. The conversation lasted about two hours, at the end of which I said, in a playful and teasing way, since I was fully aware of his ethnic origins, as he was of mine: "I never expected you to turn out to be a Jewish intellectual!" "Semitic," he said, correcting me genially. "We're *both* Semitic intellectuals."

Well, whatever. But the point I am getting at is that it

was Bill Baroody as intellectual, not simply as entrepreneur or organizer or fund-raiser—it was Bill Baroody as a man passionately interested in general ideas, and in linking these ideas to contemporary concerns—who was in good part responsible for building up the American Enterprise Institute to the eminence it possesses today. Yes, AEI has always had, as its central focus, economic policy, and especially the ways in which mischievous or mindless economic policies can debilitate the economic system on which the American democratic republic has been based since its founding, and which has contributed so much to the success of the American experiment in self-government. Even today, of course, this remains its central focus. But what has made AEI different from the other "think tanks" I have known—what has given it a special energy as well as a special temperament—is precisely this dimension of intellectual curiosity, a willingness to push beyond the more conventional limits of economic analysis.

Now, I wish it to be clearly understood that some of my best friends are economists. I have learned much from them—if much too slowly—and I look forward to learning still more from them. It really is terribly important, these days, to know a fair amount of economics. When Sir Charles Snow, in his famous lecture on "The Two Cultures," lamented the ignorance of science among literary intellectuals, humanists, and social scientists, he quite blandly overlooked the ignorance of economics among scientists and nonscientists alike. Yet I would venture to say that this ignorance of economics has been more disastrous to the world—has killed, stunted, and made miserable more people—than any ignorance of science.

And yet, critical as a knowledge of economics is for anyone interested in public policy, it remains true that those who know only economics are often astonishingly defenseless against those who attack or subvert or reject our economic system as a whole. Economists are very good at coping with specific criticisms of this system. But, more often than not, these specific criticisms are not at all specific in origin. There is an odor of bad faith—bad intellectual faith—surrounding many of these criticisms. They emerge, as it were, *post facto*—which is to say, they emerge as a consequence of a previous intellectual denial of the rationale of the system as a whole.

Anticapitalism is a hydra-headed monster against which our economists defend themselves (and us) by cutting off one head at a time. That's good work. But the trunk remains intact, and the heads grow back. It is for this reason that the defense of democratic capitalism as a whole, left largely to economists for almost two centuries now, is so much less effective than it might have been.

The problem arises because the critics of capitalism do not share certain crucial axioms on which economic science itself rests. However, such is the prestige of science in our time— even of a social science like economics—that the denial of these axioms is almost always implicit, rarely explicit. (Sometimes the denial may even be subconscious.) The upshot is that, more often than not, the economic defense of capitalism misses the point—as do so many of our current efforts at what is called "economic education." The point is that the criticisms do not flow from economic ignorance, in need of patient enlightenment. The point, rather, is that those criticisms are rooted in what might be called economic atheism—a rejection of the universe as it is perceived by economics—so that economic discourse has about as much effect as a scholarly theological sermon addressed to determined unbelievers.

Let me give two instances of what I have in mind— instances that refer to two basic axioms of economic science.

The first axiom, basic to all economic theory since Adam

Smith, is that all of us are, most of the time, and especially in our relations with strangers, irredeemably self-interested creatures. To put it another way: though we may have our angelic moments, it is absurd to try to establish an economic or political system on the assumption that such moments can envelop the totality of our lives. What democratic capitalism does is to accept the power of self-interest as a fact of life, just as it accepts the power of sex as a fact of life, or the power of political ambition as a fact of life. And what it does is to try to channel these powers—which, since they are powers, can destroy—to constructive ends. And it does so by *institutionalizing* these powers—in the market economy, in the family, in democratic politics within a framework of limited government.

But what if you decide that these are not really facts of life, that the world does not have to adapt itself to such realities, that human nature—given proper encouragement—can be totally disinterested, altruistic, absolutely fraternal and loving? What, in short, if you decide an ideal "cooperative commonwealth" would become a reality if we only effected various radical reforms? Once you have reached that conclusion, capitalism is indicted and found guilty without need of a trial, and you are then free to excoriate capitalism for any and all of the world's imperfections, which are then defined as capitalism's iniquities.

It will be said that such a point of view of human nature and of the world's inherent possibilities is utopian. Of course it is. Yet we have seen such utopianism wreak havoc among the nations and peoples of the twentieth century. And the only effective answer is to persuade people that such thinking is indeed utopian. But such persuasion is outside the province of economics, as economists will quickly agree. It is only political philosophy and history that can provide a curative disillusionment—more accurately, a liberation from illusions—for the disease of utopianism.

The second instance I would offer involves another axiom

of economics, basic to all economic theory since Adam Smith. It is that which we call "consumer sovereignty." This asserts that the ordinary man and woman, under all but extraordinary circumstances, knows his own needs better than anyone else can know them for him. Without such a principle, there would be no justification for a free market. Nor would there be any possibility of economic theory, which assumes that people know their own best interests and express this knowledge in their economic behaviors.

But what if one denies this axiom, implicitly or explicitly? What if one says that people may know what they want but are not likely to know what they need, and that a superior and authoritative wisdom should have the power to supply them with what they need, regardless of what they think they want? In fact, it is this counter-axiom that has seemed "natural" to most human societies prior to the advent of modern capitalism. It is this counter-axiom that is fundamental to all socialist societies. And one does have the impression that it is a point of view not uncongenial to fairly large numbers of people here in our own Washington, D.C.

Here again, as with the *utopian illusion,* so with the *authoritarian impulse*—economics is helpless in confronting it, as economists will quickly agree. It is only the study of political theory and political history that will vindicate capitalism's original and unique faith in the good sense of the common man and common woman, while engendering skepticism about the wisdom of benevolent despotism.

It is to Bill Baroody's eternal credit that he understood how important it is to go beyond economics to political philosophy or religious thought if we are to win the intellectual battle that swirls around democratic capitalism today—if we are indeed to "revitalize" America. It is this understanding that has brought so many political and social theorists—myself included—into close association with AEI. I should like to think we have helped, if only a bit, to make AEI somewhat more intellectually exciting than it otherwise would have been. And if we have failed to measure up to Bill's expectations—well, at least we have all learned some economics, as Bill, in his wisdom, fully intended we should.

WILLIAM J. BAROODY, SR.

Remembered by
Michael Novak

Let me begin with a story Mr. Baroody liked. A short while before I came to AEI, I was invited down to Houston to lecture to a group of oilmen, who had just been publicly accused of being greedy, selfish, and evil. It made a poor professor of theology, I said, feel like Jesus in the presence of "publicans and sinners." Three weeks later, the transcript came back "*RE*-publicans and sinners." Which, as a lifelong Democrat, was all right by me. For tonight's purpose, that should include almost all of us.

I told that story to Mr. Baroody. He said to me with a twinkle: "Michael, let me tell you something about sin. That's where the majority is."

I have since thought that this was the Baroody angle on the Jerry Falwell principle: Democracy, capitalism, and a pluralistic culture are designed for a sinful, not-quite-so-moral majority.

William J. Baroody, Sr., was the first leader of a public policy think tank to grasp the importance of religion in public affairs. Perhaps he understood this so clearly because his own heritage placed him near the historical center of Judaism, Christianity, and Islam. He understood the sense of tragedy. He understood sin. He understood hope. He understood the depths that move the world.

Our literary culture in recent generations has been rather chastely secular. Undeterred, Mr. Baroody studied the tides of family, culture, religion, and moral tradition which well up unseen around the world.

For that reason, he wished to concentrate some of the scarce resources of the American Enterprise Institute on the hidden movements of religion and philosophy roiling below the gaze of most public policy analysts. The moment was none too soon. In Iran and Nicaragua, Lebanon and Israel, Poland and the United States, religion has broken through the surface. It has done so even in secular disguise. Not many generations ago, preachers used to predict the end of the world. Today professors of environmental science do so. Some persons have thought that "liberation" and "consciousness-raising" have weakened America's Puritan moral fiber. Mr. Baroody observed that the truly liberated Puritans of today still flog themselves—by jogging.

Under the assaults of surface change, Mr. Baroody had a finely tuned Middle Eastern serenity. He knew the world might end badly. But he rather expected it to muddle through for another thousand years or so.

He believed in ideas. He believed our system needed ideas worthy of it. He thought our practice better than our theories. For the social system of the United States, he liked the name "democratic capitalism." Such a system, he saw, was in effect in all too few of the one hundred and fifty-six or so nations of the world—not more than twenty or thirty.

He saw our system as three systems in one: a political system, an economic system, a moral-cultural system, each with a certain independence of the other two, yet all three interdependent.

Our system is a political system: democratic; based upon rights, and perhaps particularly the right of each person to pursue his or her own happiness; conceived in liberty and justice. It is a political experiment, testing whether any system so conceived can long endure.

It is also an economic system: as independent from the state as is the church; free; committed predominantly, though not entirely, to markets; offering incentives. It is a system communal in its aims. It is aimed not at the wealth of individuals nor at the wealth of Scotland or Great Britain but—in Adam Smith's telling phrase—at *The Wealth of Nations*, all nations. It is communal in its systemic intention, to improve the material lot of all humankind. It is communal in its distinctive invention, the private corporation, and in the wide range of social skills in which it instructs all its citizens—even the seven-year-olds whose busy social lives demand more drivers than any two parents can supply.

It is, thirdly, a moral-cultural system. Deliberately, the Founders of this triple system separated the church from the state—and not only the church but the universities, the press, the research institutes, and, in general, the entire competition of ideas among its citizens.

The fact that there are three systems, not just one, naturally introduces "cultural contradictions" into democratic capitalism. These are deliberate. The demands of realistic politics are not the same as the demands of realistic economics. The bite of moral and cultural commitments, which our citizens feel in different and plural ways, makes economic and political consensus extremely difficult. Deliberately so.

The Founders of our system did not trust the will-to-power in any one of these three systems. That is why they divided the systems. Those who rise to the top of one of these systems seldom completely understand the other two. Those who dwell mostly in the moral-cultural system may not be able to understand the symbols on the financial pages of the newspapers— and still live perfectly happy lives. It seems to be required that those who rise to the top of the political system know little about economics. Those at the top of the economic system are often baffled by the political system, and too busy to know much about what the theologians, philosophers, poets, or artists are doing.

The system is based upon a profound distrust of the will-to-power in human beings. That is why, some think, the Founders chose a precious motto. It is embossed now on our coins: "In God we trust." Meaning: Nobody else. The three systems are *supposed* to watch each other like hawks—and temperaments attracted to each are not expected to like temperaments attracted to the others. Political leaders do not actually have to *like* businessmen, economists, journalists, academics, and the like— nor are the others expected to like each other. Civil hostility is quite in order. (If love were easy, why would it be commanded?)

Such a system is Jewish, Christian, humanistic in its hope that a free people, given a system mirroring the natural demands of liberty, may create a brilliant testament to the capacities of human beings for justice, compassion, and decency.

Our political system cannot survive apart from moral commitments to justice, personal responsibility, and self-government. Our economic system makes no sense apart from a willingness to cooperate with one another; to take risks together; freely to join one another's labors; and to defer satisfactions in order to invest in the future. No society can enjoy our form of politics or our form of economics unless it has a moral culture analogous to ours.

Mr. Baroody heard with his inner ear the voice of pessimists, like Joseph Schumpeter, who reluctantly thought our system would probably destroy itself. Such pessimists seldom believe destruction will come because our political system is less free or less just than any other. They do not believe it will perish because our economic system produces less or distributes it less widely than any other. Nearly all of them point to a flaw in our moral-cultural system. They fear that it will generate an adversarial culture whose resentments and illusions will lead us like the Gadarene swine over a precipice. They fear that economic and political success will break our people's tie with reality and destroy us in the pursuit of illusions. There are many signs that unrealistic ideas are making our politics difficult and crippling our economics. When the idea gets around that graduates of Harvard may collect unemployment checks in hardship locations like Aspen, Fort Lauderdale, and Paris, burdens are placed upon the political system and the economic system which, in the long run, they cannot bear. Ideas can destroy as well as build.

Such a failure is not commanded by the stars. If our society's fatal flaw lies not in our political system, nor in our economic system, but in our ideas and in our visions, there is something we can do about it. Nothing obliges us to destroy ourselves. We may combat destructive ideas with good ideas. We may heed what Pascal describes as the first of all moral obligations: to think clearly.

Mr. Baroody entered the war of ideas with zest and relish. He loved the clash of opposites. He believed in ideas in competition. Where stand-offs ensued, he believed in going deeper.

It may be, as the pessimists think, that our system, which appeared in history only a short time ago, will soon disappear like a comet in the dark. Well it may. We are being tested, these days, as often before. Once again on Poland's borders tanks rumble. Liberty is under threat. Liberty is scarcer in the darkness of this world than oil.

Thus immigrants continue to seek these shores, as Mr. Baroody's parents did and many of our parents. On the Statue of Liberty are carved words not unlike those which Mr. Baroody especially loved, from the Easter Sermon of St. John Chrysostom, words which were read when Mr. Baroody's battle with cancer had subdued him and death had taken him from us:

> You the first and you the last: equally heaped with blessings. You the rich and you the poor: celebrate together. You the careful and you the careless: enjoy this day of days. You that have kept the fast, and you that have broken it: be happy today. . . . Feed sumptuously all: feed on his goodness, his sheer abundance. No one need think he is poor, for the universal empire is emblazoned, wide open for all.

That empire is the empire of liberty. In heaven, it is the crystalline City of God. In this ambiguous world, liberty rests upon the strength of a triple system—a free polity, a free economy, a free moral-cultural order. Messy, but doable.

Realism in economics and realism in politics depend on realism in religion and philosophy. Mr. Baroody was an archer of unerring aim. He loved politics. He loved economics. But he aimed a favorite arrow at the moral heart of our system.

He struck us each in our hearts.

Additional remarks by
Ronald W. Reagan

Since November 4, the focus of myself and members of my staff has been almost exclusively a forward one. We have been planning and working on the transition and, in many ways, our concerns are those addressed in AEI's Public Policy Week— What are the possibilities of revitalizing America? We will be looking closely at AEI's observations and proposals. Many of my staff have been with AEI, and we of the next administration want to maintain this kind of working relationship with AEI during the next four years.

I have had something of a revitalizing experience myself during the past few weeks. For a reason that I think is fairly obvious, I have been spending my time reading inaugural addresses by past presidents. It is remarkable how consistently the theme of American history has been played out in those addresses. What struck me in particular were the constant references to the role that Providence has played in blessing this land and the equally consistent references to the virtue and the vigor of the American people as our greatest national resource.

In discussing questions about revitalizing our country,

we should keep these two themes in mind. In our troubled century, the concept of self-government, under God, remains the beginning and the end of political wisdom. No one knew that better than Bill Baroody. He devoted his life to recovering the great concepts of Western culture and revitalizing them for our modern age.

Nick Thimmesch quotes Bill Baroody, Sr., whose memory we are gathered here to honor, as saying, "I've always felt that a sound idea, soundly pursued will ultimately challenge the prevailing wisdom and make its mark." Well, Bill Baroody made his mark and it will be a lasting one.

According to a *Washington Star* editorial, Bill Baroody decided back in the 1950s that the New Deal dogma on politics and economics had run out of steam, leaving a clear track for a vigorous new kind of conservatism. Bill Baroody was right, and some of us who might have thought back in the 1950s that we were alone in that belief were wrong. One of Bill Baroody's greatest accomplishments was in building an institution that said, "Here is a place where you can develop your ideas," that said to others, "Here is a place you can turn to for advice," that said to all of us who were concerned about our country's future, "You are not alone." He would have been the first to acknowledge that, like any of us, he couldn't do it alone, and that like the luckiest of us he had the best of friends to work with—the first being, of course, his wife, Bee, who must be so proud tonight.

And, of course, there were so many others, only one of whom I'll mention tonight, both because he was a special friend of Bill's and because he is a special friend of mine. I was reminded only recently that they went to AEI together, and only when the work there was well begun did Glenn Campbell come out West to head the Hoover Institution.

The competition of ideas that Bill Baroody spoke of so often has not been won, but those of us who have different ideas about government and public policy have been given a chance to prove that there are better ideas for governing America—that negotiating arms limitation from a position of military strength is better than just negotiating arms limitation; that having government social programs that can help the poor move away from dependency on others is better than having programs that are elaborate handouts; that seeking to balance the federal budget while stimulating savings and rewarding personal initiative by lowering taxes at the same time is better than just trying to balance the budget.

"Family" was one of the watchwords of the election campaign. I understand that many of you here once were characterized by Bill Baroody, Jr., as members of Bill, Sr.'s larger family and that the kinship he referred to was not of blood but of faith in the importance of ideas.

I ask you all to keep that faith and to continue the search for better ideas and ways to put them to work. For those of you who think that's an important part of the job of revitalizing America, let me borrow a page from Bill Baroody's book and remind you, you're not alone.

RONALD W. REAGAN / 37

Additional remarks by
Gerald R. Ford

It is a high honor and privilege to be here on this occasion, the Fourth Annual Boyer Dinner. Let me say that, since January 20, 1977, I have been very fortunate in having an excellent relationship with AEI, through Bill Baroody, Jr. I have visited sixty-four college and university campuses, taught more than five hundred classes, and answered some five thousand questions from students and faculty. Let me tell you, that's an invigorating, challenging experience; I survived.

Over the many, many years I knew Bill Baroody, Sr., our relationship couldn't have been better. It was superb in every way; I cherished our friendship. God bless his family in the years ahead.

Last month, something happened that Bill Baroody might have foreseen. I just wish that he could have been here on November 4, 1980. Although we cannot yet be sure of the full impact of the elections this year, it does appear that something very, very big happened. As I interpret it, Americans at the polls spoke with a voice that was loud and clear. They want a change of direction and a change of philosophy in their federal government.

They have called upon a new president and new men and women in the Congress of the United States to employ new ideas, based upon older values and older principles, to meet the particular challenges of our time, in the decade of the 1980s.

In my judgment, they have chosen well, and I do not believe they will be disappointed. But whether or not I'm right depends, in large measure, on how well the preparations have been made for the leaders who are coming in to take advantage of this new and unique opportunity.

During the last thirty years, the period of my experience in public life, many of us worked to hold the line, to prevent a more state-centered philosophy from becoming too deeply entrenched and from going too far unquestioned.

During those thirty years, Bill Baroody, Sr., was there to help us in every way—helping us to hold the line, backing us up on defense. At the same time, here at AEI he was preparing an offense. In football jargon, I guess you could say that Bill Baroody was playing it both ways.

If the way is well prepared for the new leaders to offer a new approach, new ideas, and new vision for this country, no one in the postwar history of the United States deserves more credit than does Bill Baroody, who built the American Enterprise Institute into the fine and critically important institution it has become and will continue to be.

While we held the line in the Congress, Americans gradually became more attracted to the vision that Bill Baroody, and many of you here tonight, worked so hard to develop. It was the vision of an America with a people and an economy whose strengths were rooted in freedom from excessive government intervention. It was a vision of an America that recognized anew the value of what the American Enterprise Institute has come to call "mediating structures"—neighborhoods, the family, and private groups, like unions, businesses, and fraternal associations. It was the vision of an America that was strong in its understanding of its national interests, in its ability to defend those interests, and in its conviction that the American case should be made to the world without apology, and that the world would do well to listen.

That vision is the message that AEI and a few other centers of thought have tried to articulate, and it appears now to be taking hold. All of us should thank Bill Baroody for a great deal of what has happened. We're blessed to have what he built and left behind to carry on the work, the American Enterprise Institute.

It is my judgment that Bill Baroody's work and vision will continue to blossom and unfold in the days ahead.

Bill's last years were spent trying to put AEI on a solid financial ground. His work on the development drive, of which I am pleased to be the honorary chairman, was a job that Bill started well but, unfortunately, could not complete. It was the only job I ever knew Bill to start without finishing.

There were so many projects that Bill undertook, so many difficult challenges that he met. By the time he was done, though, he had made them look easy.

I still don't know how Bill Baroody did it. Only weeks before he died, when I talked to him on the phone, he explained what made him try: "I am, despite all, an optimist."

Because of the work Bill Baroody did throughout his lifetime, and because of the legacy he has left us, there is some reason for all of us to be optimists. He always understood two things—purpose and value. He believed in the moral order and the basic moral values—in his words, the values of honesty, justice, respect for property, and responsibility in public office.

He worked for value-centered education, designed to raise fundamental questions and to provide for both the material and the spirtual sides of man.

Finally, Bill Baroody never lost sight of his purpose, which was to educate—to educate by discussing, provoking, mediating, stimulating, challenging. Even near the end of his life, affected by the painful cancer, he made one last trip to educate, as the commencement speaker at Albion College, in the state of Michigan.

He warned the graduating seniors that they were shoving off into very troubled waters, but he concluded by distilling, in a very few paragraphs, his own personal philosophy. It bears repeating.

> But I am despite all an optimist. I subscribe to the belief and the vision that motivated my father to journey from distant Lebanon eighty years ago—knowing neither the language, the customs, nor the specific opportunities that might exist. Yet he came because there was a vision that this land and this nation was unique in human history—a nation with a system that permitted a man, if he were willing to work, to live a life that was fully human and provide an opportunity for his children and theirs to live an even better life.

> That is the system and the way of life which you are called upon to defend and preserve. That means involvement. That means work. That means— whether you are lawyer, teacher, businessman, doctor, or whatever—that you realize what is at stake and give it everything you have.

> And . . . it means that you must constantly remember the *importance*—*sacredness* may not be too

strong a word—of "everything you have" and have received from Albion. You have more than mere knowledge. You possess an entire civilization's legacy of values which, if we can preserve them against the current trends of attack or neglect, can in turn preserve us and the way of life we treasure.

Bill Baroody's professional life immersed him in a study of public policy. His personal life was deeply affected by his religion, which, though personal, was never kept private: it influenced everything he did. Bill Baroody was a whole man in that his personal beliefs and his public beliefs could not be in conflict. It was part of Bill's philosophy that they were and should be complementary.